Women in Business

DAVID EVANS

Level 4

Series Editors: Andy Hopkins and Jocelyn Potter

Pearson Education Limited
Edinburgh Gate, Harlow,
Essex CM20 2JE, England
and Associated Companies throughout the world.

ISBN 978-0-582-45327-2

7 9 10 8

Typeset by Pantek Arts Ltd, Maidstone, Kent
Set in 11/14pt Bembo
Printed in China
SWTC/07

Published by Pearson Education Limited in association with
Penguin Books Ltd., both companies being subsidiaries of Pearson Plc

Photograph acknowledgements:
Frank Spooner: p.2, p. 18 and p. 23; Everyday Pictures p. 9;
Rex Features: p. 26, p. 32, p. 38, p. 46 and p. 52; Kobal: p. 43.

For a complete list of titles available in the Penguin Readers series please write to your local
Pearson Education office or contact: Penguin Readers Marketing Department,
Pearson Education, Edinburgh Gate, Harlow, Essex, CM20 2JE.

Contents

Introduction

Some people are discussing the company's financial performance or its latest sales figures. But others are discussing campaigns to save the forests of Brazil or ways of helping political prisoners . . .

This building is the head office of The Body Shop, a company which was started by one woman, Anita Roddick, in 1976. In just a few years, her company has grown from one small shop into a large international business. During this time, she has shown people that business is not just about making money; she believes that business can help to make the world a better place.

For years, working women found they had little chance of getting a top job. The bosses of big business were nearly always men. They were often good at managing money but bad at managing people. Most of them were good at selling traditional products but bad at creating new ones. Many of them thought in the same way, said the same kinds of things and wore the same dark suits.

But in recent years, business has changed. There are now opportunities for people to think differently and to manage companies in new ways. At last, women have been able to test new ideas and try new ways of working. Although many women still have problems in the workplace, more and more are reaching the top in their business lives.

This book tells the stories of five women from very different backgrounds who have reached the top in very different ways. They have all succeeded by using their special skills to create completely new kinds of companies.

Chapter 1   Coco Chanel

'Fashion is not just about dresses; fashion is something in the air. Fashion is in the sky, the street. Fashion is about ideas, the way we live, what is happening.'

Coco Chanel

At the start of the twentieth century, the idea of women in business seemed crazy. In those days, men held all the positions of power and made all the decisions about money. They believed that a woman's place was in the home, looking after her children, cooking for her family and managing the house. If a woman needed to work she could perhaps find a job in a shop or in a factory, but she had no chance of working as a businesswoman or a banker or a lawyer.

Women's fashions in the US and Europe at that time supported this idea of their position in society. Fashionable women wore long dresses that almost touched the ground. This made it difficult for them to drive a car, ride a horse or even walk quickly. As a result, they needed men to arrange their travel for them. A fashionable woman was also expected to keep her skin as white as possible to show that she didn't work outside in the sun. This meant that women spent a lot of time indoors. When they went out, they often wore large hats that were decorated with flowers, leaves and fruit. These protected their faces from the sun and made it even more difficult for them to move around.

But many women weren't happy with their position in society, and they didn't like the clothes they had to wear either. One of these people was a Frenchwoman called Gabrielle 'Coco' Chanel. When she went into business in 1910, she planned to

1

Gabrielle 'Coco' Chanel

change the clothes that women wore. But over the next sixty years she did much more than that, as she became the richest and most successful businesswoman of the century.

◆

Coco Chanel had no experience of business when she opened her first hat shop in Paris in 1910. She was only twenty-seven years old and she came from an ordinary family. When she left school, she worked for a dressmaker for a short time. Later she tried to become a singer in a nightclub, where she was given the name 'Coco'. Coco was an attractive young woman; she always dressed well and she was good at making friends. Although she didn't have any money, she mixed with fashionable, successful people and her boyfriends were often rich young army officers. One of these was a handsome young Englishman with a big black moustache, called Boy Capel. When Coco asked him to lend her some money so she could open a shop, he was surprised. He had never heard of a woman in business before, but he liked the idea.

'A woman in business?' he said. 'That sounds fun. How much do you want?'

Coco asked for enough money to open a shop in one of the best streets in Paris.

'No problem,' replied Boy Capel. He was so rich that he didn't care if he never got his money back.

Many of Coco's customers in her first shop were her rich young women friends. They loved the simple but beautiful hats that Coco made for them. At parties they laughed at other women who still wore hats that were covered in fruit and flowers. Soon they were asking Coco for clothes that were designed in the same simple way. Coco hated the long dresses that fashionable women wore and so she was happy to make dresses and skirts that were much shorter and reached just below the knee. She also persuaded her customers to wear loose jackets and blouses that allowed them to breathe more easily. Again, the rich, fashionable young women of Paris loved Coco's new ideas, and her shop started to do well.

In 1913, Coco asked Boy Capel for more money, because she wanted to open a second shop, this time in the French seaside town of Deauville. In summer, the streets of Deauville were full of fashionable people from all over Europe. Russian princesses mixed with English ladies and the daughters of German businessmen, and they were all looking for clothes in the latest style. After her success in Paris, Coco was sure she could offer all of them something special. She was right. The young women in Deauville loved her simple hats, loose jackets, and skirts and dresses that reached just below the knee. Coco made plenty of money in her first year in Deauville and in her second summer she expected to do even better. But then, for everyone in Europe, everything went wrong.

In June 1914 in Sarajevo, Bosnia, a young student called Gavrilo Princep shot and killed Archduke Franz Ferdinand, an important person in the Austrian royal family. Two months later, almost all the nations of Europe were fighting one of the worst wars in history. In August of that year, the German army marched through Belgium and into the north of France. The French army was not prepared for this, and soldiers rushed to defend their country. The British army quickly came to help, but the situation looked very dangerous.

Many rich French families rushed from the north of France to the expensive hotels of Deauville to get away from the fighting. Some people were frightened, but most were in a good mood.

'Don't worry,' they told each other. 'The war will be finished by Christmas.'

But after a few weeks, it was clear that they were wrong. More and more men left Deauville to go and fight in the French army. Soon the expensive hotels were changed into hospitals, full of soldiers who had been hurt in the fighting. The rich Frenchwomen of Deauville saw that it was their duty to help the French army and many of them took jobs as nurses in the hospitals or did other kinds of war work. But after a few days they realized that it was impossible to work in their long dresses. They looked around for different things to wear.

'Where can we find clothes that are stylish, but will also allow us to work?' they asked each other.

They found the answer in Coco Chanel's new shop. Her simple hats, loose jackets and straight skirts were just what these women needed. They were stylish, but they also allowed women to move around quickly. Coco was soon selling clothes as fast as she could make them.

A year later, in the summer of 1915, Coco had worked so hard for so long that she was ready for a holiday. So Boy Capel took a break from his job with the British army, and together they went to Biarritz in the south of France. The mood in this seaside town was very different to the mood in Deauville. In Deauville, everyone spent all their time worrying about the war; in Biarritz, people just wanted to have a good time and to forget about it. The town was full of young army officers who were spending a few days away from the fighting with their wives and girlfriends. There was dancing in the big hotels every night. The shops and restaurants were always busy. But the war meant that it was hard for women in Biarritz to find the sort of fashionable clothes that they wanted. Coco immediately saw a business opportunity.

She realized that women in Biarritz wanted a different style of clothes from women in Deauville. These women wanted to go out and have fun. They wanted to look good and they didn't really care how much they paid for their clothes.

'Don't you see?' she said to Boy. 'This could be a new direction for the business. In Biarritz I can sell clothes that are modern and simple, but that also allow women to feel beautiful and to enjoy themselves.'

Boy Capel put his fingers to his big black moustache and thought for a moment.

'And,' added Coco, 'I think women will also pay a very good price for these clothes, if we can sell them in the right way.'

'What do you mean?' asked Boy.

'Well,' said Coco, 'these clothes need to have a new look. The Chanel clothes in Biarritz will not just be clothes for rich women who work. These clothes will make women feel good when they wear them.'

Boy wasn't sure about the idea. 'But where will you get the cloth for these clothes?' he asked. 'No other designer can get cloth at the moment. We are in the middle of a war, you know.'

'Don't worry about that,' said Coco, 'I'll find the cloth. I just need the money.'

'Money?' said Boy Capel. 'Oh, no problem. I've got plenty of money.'

Boy Capel sounded confident, but as he lent more money to Coco, he never really expected to see it again.

But Coco's idea was quite right. She found that she could still buy cloth across the border in Spain, which wasn't fighting in the war. Then she rented an expensive house in the middle of the town and hired sixty women to make her new dresses. She sold the dresses for very high prices, but women were happy to pay for them. They were so popular that people even came from Madrid to buy them.

For the next three years, Coco travelled between her three businesses in Paris, Deauville and Biarritz, while the First World War continued in the north and east of France. By 1916, over three hundred people were working for her. She soon made so much money that she could pay back Boy Capel all that she had borrowed. Coco had been lucky because the war had given her a chance to make her new designs popular. But she had also shown that she could recognize business opportunities and that she could change her style to suit her customers.

When the war finished, in November 1918, Coco was ready to start the next and most successful part of her business life.

◆

The First World War completely changed European society. Millions of young men had been killed, and women now had a much more important position in society. Women had shown that they could work in offices and factories while men were fighting in the war. In many countries, women were now allowed to vote for their government for the first time. By the start of the 1920s, women had realized that they could be different from their mothers. They could lead a very different kind of life from the one they had known before the war.

After the bad times of the war, rich young people just wanted to spend money and to have fun. They drove their shiny new cars to the beach, where they played games and swam in the sea. Both men and women went to parties, where they smoked cigarettes and drank alcohol. They danced to the music of Louis Armstrong and Jelly Roll Morton. They went to the cinema to watch the films of Charlie Chaplin and Greta Garbo. And they also wore the clothes of Coco Chanel.

Women didn't want to return to the long, tight dresses and silly hats of the years before the war. They wanted clothes that allowed them to move around freely. Chanel's style was just right for the time. But now her clothes were not just for the women of Paris, Deauville and Biarritz. The end of the war meant that she could sell her clothes around the world. For women in the big cities of Europe, she made smart suits of jackets and skirts, and for women on holiday she designed special beach clothes. In the US her dresses were so successful that a magazine even compared them to the Ford motor car. Coco's business grew and grew.

But Coco didn't just think about clothes. She realized that women couldn't always wear diamonds and other expensive jewellery when they went out. So she started making jewellery that looked real, but was made from cheap materials. She also introduced the idea of short hair for women, and for the first time she made it popular for women to go out in the sun so their skin went brown.

But Coco's best decision was to go into the cosmetics business. She knew that the cosmetics business and the fashion industry were similar in many ways, and she was sure that her ideas could help her to be successful in this area. She also believed that cosmetics were very important. She once said, 'If a woman doesn't wear perfume, she has no future.'

So in the early 1920s, she went to see a man called Pierre Wertheimer to discuss her plan. Wertheimer owned the biggest perfume factory in France and he was very happy to work with such a famous designer. At that time women wore perfumes which always smelled of flowers, but Coco wanted her perfume to have a completely different smell. Together Wertheimer and Chanel invented a new kind of perfume, and they decided to sell it in a simple, square bottle. They agreed to give it Coco's name, and she added her lucky number. The result was Chanel No.* 5, the most successful perfume of the past hundred years.

As Coco grew richer and more successful, she mixed with the most famous people of the time. She loved to be with artists and she made clothes for shows at theatres in Paris, where she worked with Jean Cocteau, Pablo Picasso and Sergei Diaghilev. These people all admired Coco's work and understood what she was trying to do.

'Coco worked in fashion according to rules that seem to have value only for painters, musicians and writers,' said Jean Cocteau.

*No.: a short form of 'number'.

8

Chanel No.5, the most successful perfume
of the past hundred years.

But Coco didn't just mix with artists. She often went to parties where she met important people like the future King of England – the Prince of Wales – and Britain's future war leader, Winston Churchill. And after her boyfriend of the war years, Boy Capel, was killed in a car crash, she was often seen on the arm of rich Russian and English lords.

For Coco and her friends, the 1920s were the happiest ten years of the twentieth century. But the good times suddenly ended in October 1929, when the stock exchange in Wall Street, New York, crashed. Share prices fell and fell and fell. The world economy was badly damaged. Thousands of businesses closed and millions of people lost their jobs.

For most people, the Wall Street crash was a disaster, but not for Coco Chanel. While ordinary people suffered, the richest people in the world still had money and they still wanted expensive, fashionable clothes. Instead of making cheaper, simpler clothes, she started to design even more expensive clothes and to use real diamonds in her jewellery. Coco had remembered the lesson of Biarritz: in times of trouble, the secret of success is to help people to forget their problems.

In these bad times for the world economy, other successful people remembered the same secret. One of these people was the great Hollywood film producer, Sam Goldwyn. As ordinary people in America got poorer and poorer, he realized that they wanted to see films about a different kind of world. They wanted films that showed the wonderful lives of rich, beautiful people. They wanted to go to the cinema and get away from their problems. Goldwyn decided that people in his films should wear the best and the most expensive clothes in the world, and so he went to the top fashion designer in the world: Coco Chanel. Coco understood his idea immediately and she was interested.

'How much will you pay me?' she asked.

'One million dollars,' said Goldwyn.

With an offer of so much money, how could Coco refuse? She went to Hollywood, she met the film stars, and then she started work on their clothes. Everyone waited to see the results. The first film was called *Tomorrow Or Never* and its star was Gloria Swanson. In the film her clothes were beautiful, but they were quite simple. When the film was shown in the US, people were surprised; they had expected something more for $1 million. When an American newspaper wrote about the film it said, 'Chanel wants a lady to look like a lady; Hollywood wants a lady to look like two ladies.'

Chanel kept the money, but Sam Goldwyn decided not to use her clothes again.

Back in Paris, Coco had more problems. The French economy was in a very bad state. People without work wanted jobs, and the people with jobs wanted more money. Bosses like Coco had everything, while it was hard for many French people to feed their families. In the middle of the 1930s, Coco's business employed around 4,000 people. She thought she was good to the people who worked for her, but some of them had a different opinion. In 1936, fifty of her workers stopped work and sat down in one of her factories in Paris. Coco put on her best suit and rushed to speak to them, but they had locked the door of her factory and she couldn't get in. Coco was very angry. How could they do this to her? She and her workers argued and argued, but they couldn't agree on a solution to their differences. Coco's reply showed that she was a very tough businesswoman: she sacked three hundred of them. But still they refused to change their minds. Coco now had an even more serious problem. She had designed some new clothes for a fashion show and she was worried that they wouldn't be ready. What could she do? She decided to give her workers what they wanted, but she never forgot what they had done to her.

At around this time, Coco started to go out with a rich

German man called Hans Günther von Dincklage. She always called him 'von D'. Nobody knew exactly what von D was doing in Paris, but many people thought that he was a spy for Germany's Nazi government. This didn't worry Coco, and the two of them started to live together in the expensive Paris Ritz Hotel.

But while Coco and von D enjoyed their life, Europe moved closer to war. In 1938, Hitler's German army marched into Czechoslovakia. The next year, the Germans marched into Poland and the Second World War began.

Although Coco's business had done well in the First World War, she decided that she didn't want to work through another war. Perhaps she was still angry with her workers after the problems of 1936. Or perhaps she had just had enough of business. But for whatever reason, in 1939 Coco closed her fashion business and all her workers lost their jobs. Many people were angry with her and asked her to change her mind, but she simply told them, 'This is no time for fashion.'

Through the winter of 1939 and into 1940, the French people waited and worried. In 1940, the German army arrived and took control of Paris. Many French people started secret groups and continued to fight the Germans, but not Coco. She was happy in her rooms at the Ritz Hotel with her German boyfriend, and she just wanted to enjoy her life. The war hadn't closed the theatres and shops of Paris, so she could still go out and do what she wanted. But as her fashion business was now closed, she needed to find other ways of making money.

She knew that her perfume Chanel No. 5 was still very popular with the French and German women who were living in Paris. She also knew that her partner in the perfume business, Pierre Wertheimer, had left France to get away from the war and was now living in the US. Coco thought she saw an opportunity to take control of the whole perfume business. But although Wertheimer was on the other side of the Atlantic, he was not going to allow this to happen. Chanel No. 5 made him so much money that he didn't want to lose control of it. Coco, Wertheimer and their lawyers started to argue about it.

But while Coco and Wertheimer fought for control of Chanel No. 5, the Germans were slowly losing control of the war. In June 1944, the British and the Americans landed on the beaches of the west of France and started to move towards Paris. Two months later, they were just outside the city. The Germans realized that they were beaten and started to leave. The people of Paris opened the doors of their houses, had parties and danced in the streets. But Coco wasn't so happy. She knew that many French people were angry with people who had helped the Germans in the war and they wanted to punish them. Would they want to punish Coco? She wasn't going to wait to find out. When the war ended, she left France and went to live abroad.

◆

For most of the next eight years, Coco lived quietly in Switzerland. She soon found out that she was so rich that she didn't need to work. She continued to argue with Pierre Wertheimer about the control of Chanel No. 5 from her new Swiss home. But when he returned to France after the war, they found a way to solve their problems. Wertheimer kept control of the perfume business, but he agreed to pay Coco 2% of the money from sales of the perfume around the world. This meant that Coco was now earning around $1 million a year and she didn't even have to get out of bed in the morning!

As the years passed, some people still remembered the beautiful Chanel clothes from the years before the war; but they soon forgot the rich old lady who had designed them. Although Coco now had everything that she wanted, she didn't really like her new life. She had loved her work and now she missed the world of fashion. She still read fashion magazines and looked carefully at all the new designs. But Coco found that more and more often she didn't like what she saw.

The new star designer in the fashion world was a Frenchman called Christian Dior. In 1947, he produced his 'New Look'. His shirts and jackets were tight and made it difficult for women to breathe. His skirts and dresses were narrow at the waist and wide at the bottom and they reached down to women's shoes. Women loved Dior's clothes. They were very different to the boring clothes and uniforms that they had had to wear during the war years. They were also very different to the Chanel look of the years before the war.

Every year, Christian Dior's 'New Look' made Coco more and more angry. In 1953, she decided that she couldn't sit and watch and do nothing. She had to return to the fashion business. She returned to Paris and started to design new clothes for a fashion show the next year. Many people thought she was crazy.

'What does a seventy-year-old woman know about modern fashion?' they asked. 'Doesn't she know that times have changed?'

But Coco didn't listen and on 5 February 1954, she introduced her new designs at a fashion show in Paris. The show was a disaster. The newspapers said that they were clothes for old ladies and country people. Coco was upset and angry that her designs had been criticized so strongly.

'These people just don't understand,' she said. 'It's true that I'm old, but I'm still one of the greatest designers in the world. I changed women's fashion once and I know I can change it again. I'll show them!'

So Coco didn't return to Switzerland and she didn't stop working. The next year, she produced some different designs for another fashion show and this time many people liked them. The year after that, there was another new show and more and more people started to admire her clothes. By the end of the 1950s, she was again one of the most important fashion designers in the world.

During the 1960s, rich and beautiful women from all over the world visited Coco's offices to ask for advice and to buy new suits and skirts and dresses. Coco was rich and successful, but nobody really knew if she was happy. For the final seventeen years of her life, she lived alone in the Ritz Hotel in Paris. Every morning she walked across the road to work in the offices above one of her shops. She was often still cutting cloth and making dresses late at night. Why did she work so hard? She once said, 'Work has always been a kind of drug for me.'

If work was her drug, it was a drug that helped her to live for a long time. She was still designing new clothes for the world's top women when she died in 1971. She was eighty-seven years old.

◆

Today, 'Chanel' is still one of the most important names in fashion and cosmetics, but the modern 'House of Chanel' is very different to Coco's old company. A new boss, the German designer Karl Lagerfeld, joined the company in 1983 and introduced several new ideas. He saw that the company could use Chanel's famous name to sell many different products all over the world. Soon the company had shops in over forty countries. The Chanel name was on hats, belts, jewellery, clothes and handbags, as well as on many different kinds of cosmetics. Chanel's products were bought by many more women than ever before.

But if Coco were still alive today she would probably be pleased with many things about the modern company. She could walk into the best shop in any big city in the world and buy her Chanel No. 5 perfume and it would still be in the same square bottle. She could walk into a Chanel shop and still find smart suits and beautiful dresses in the simple Chanel tradition. In her work as a designer, Coco Chanel loved simple styles because she believed that a woman was always more important than the dress that she wore.

'Dress badly,' she once said, 'and people will notice the dress. Dress well and people will notice the woman.'

In her life, people noticed Coco Chanel not just because of wonderful clothes, but also because she was the first and most successful international businesswoman of the twentieth century.

Chapter 2   Hanae Mori

'I entered a world, the world of fashion, where women had little place.'
                                                              Hanae Mori

One afternoon in 1961, a young Japanese woman called Hanae
Mori arrived at the offices of the great fashion designer, Coco
Chanel, in Paris. Hanae was nervous. She had always admired the
pictures of Chanel's clothes that she had seen in fashion
magazines at home in Japan. She had also read a lot about Chanel
and knew that she was a person with very strong opinions. Now
Hanae was going to ask Chanel to design a suit for her. As she sat
and waited for her meeting, Hanae watched the women in the
office come and go. Some wore stylish Chanel suits, others wore
skirts and loose blouses with lots of beautiful jewellery.

'What kind of clothes will Chanel suggest for me?' Hanae
wondered.

At last, Chanel's door opened and Hanae went in to meet the
great designer. Hanae was surprised when she first saw her.
Chanel was much smaller than she had expected. And although
she was now an old woman in her seventies, Hanae could easily
imagine her as a beautiful young woman many years before.

Chanel looked at Hanae carefully and then said, 'You have
wonderful black hair. We must dress you in orange like the sun.'

Hanae thought for a moment. She didn't want to be rude to
such an important woman, but she didn't agree with her at all.

'I'm not sure about that,' she said. 'I like quiet colours.'

The two women discussed it for a few minutes and then
decided that Chanel would make Hanae a black suit with orange
at the edges.

Hanae Mori

When Hanae left Chanel's offices, she knew that she had bought a suit that was just right for her character. But she had also got something much more important from her meeting with Chanel. Hanae had realized that she wanted to be a designer like Coco Chanel. Before she met Chanel, she had always thought that designer fashion was a man's world. Now she knew that if Coco Chanel could succeed, then she could too.

Hanae went back to Tokyo and two years later started her own design company. Within thirty years, it had grown into a five-billion-dollar business.

♦

When Hanae met Coco Chanel in 1961, she already had a lot of experience of the clothes business, although she had never worked in designer fashion before. Her interest in clothes had started when she was a child in a small village in Shimane in the south-west of Japan. Her family was traditional in many ways, but her rich father liked his children to be dressed in the latest European styles. Little Hanae always felt very different from the other village children who arrived at school in their simple Japanese clothes, while she wore an expensive suit from Paris or London.

As she grew up, Hanae often argued with her father about her future. He wanted her to be like him and to become a doctor, but Hanae wanted to study art.

'Art?' her father used to say. 'Art is a wonderful hobby, but it's not a real subject to study.'

In the end they agreed that Hanae would study literature, and so she left her family and started a course in Japanese literature at university in Tokyo. But before she could finish her studies, the Second World War started. Like many other women students, Hanae had to stop studying and go to work in a factory. Soon she realized that the war was going badly for Japan. Every night she heard the American planes in the air above Tokyo and she listened for the sound of the explosions as the bombs fell in the city around her.

When the war ended in 1946, Japan had a lot of problems. Many of its cities had been destroyed, and millions of its people had been killed. But Hanae wanted to return to normal as quickly as possible. So she went back to university and finished her studies in 1947. At that time there seemed little chance that she would go into business.

The year before, Hanae had fallen in love with a rich young man called Ken Mori, whose family owned a factory that made cloth. They were soon married and it seemed that Hanae would become a housewife. Until the end of the Second World War, Japan had been a very traditional society and a woman was simply expected to be a good wife and a wise mother. At first, Hanae was ready to accept this situation.

'I had no problem with becoming a housewife,' she said. But it was soon clear that a life at home, looking after her husband and her family, was not for her. After just a few months, Hanae was bored. She started looking around for something to keep her busy.

In the late 1940s, Japanese society was slowly changing. In 1946, Japanese women had been allowed to vote for the first time and a few women had become politicians in Japan's parliament. There were still very few Japanese businesswomen, but if women could become politicians, why couldn't they also become successful in other areas? Hanae decided to try business.

She had always been interested in clothes, she loved art and she was married to a man who owned a cloth factory. So the clothes business was the obvious choice for her. Over the next two years, she learnt about designing clothes, cutting cloth, selling clothes and running a business. By 1951, she felt that she was ready to make and sell her own clothes. She started in a small way, making clothes for a few people, but then she had a piece of luck. An important Japanese film producer saw one of her designs and loved it. He called Hanae.

'Could you make some clothes for my next film?' he asked.

Hanae said 'yes' without even thinking about it.

Over the next six years, she made clothes for many Japanese films and worked with people like Yasujiro Ozu and Nagisa Oshima. In Japan it was a time when people were building the economy again after the war. They had high hopes for the future, and when they went to the cinema they wanted to see film stars who looked bright, strong and confident. Hanae's clothes for Japan's stars caught this mood perfectly. Her experience of working in the film industry was very important for her.

'My eyes were opened to the world,' she said. 'I understood that there were many different types of women. I realized how men looked at women and how they loved them.'

By the time she arrived in Paris for her meeting with Coco Chanel, Hanae already knew a lot about the clothes business and had made a lot of money from it. But her move into designer fashion in the early 1960s was something quite new for her.

◆

When Hanae returned from Paris, she travelled to New York to study European and American design. Then in 1965, she opened a shop in Tokyo to sell her own designer clothes. As Hanae's business grew over the next few years, she noticed that the fashion industry was changing in important ways. Coco Chanel had always designed clothes specially for each customer; when Hanae Mori bought her suit from Chanel in 1961, she knew that she was buying something that had been made just for her. But the younger designers of the late 1960s were more interested in making clothes that were ready to wear. These could be produced in much larger quantities, which allowed fashion designers to expand their businesses. Now they could have many shops in countries all round the world. As a result, designer fashion became much more international.

Hanae was very comfortable with this change, because from the start of her work in designer fashion, she wanted to make sure that her business was international. She had her first fashion show in New York in 1965, and in the 1970s she started to have regular fashion shows in Paris too. The most important part of Hanae's business has probably always been in Japan, where she now has over seventy shops. But she also has three shops in Paris, and customers can buy her clothes in over a hundred places in the US.

She has also always tried to mix Eastern and Western ideas in her designs. She designed long dresses in a Western style which were covered with Japanese writing. She liked to use cloth which was decorated with Eastern pictures of flowers and birds. She made suits in a European style, but with collars like the ones worn by China's Mao Zedong. In Japan, rich women loved her ideas and found that they could wear her clothes for all occasions: business, sport and parties. One of Hanae's greatest moments was the design of a wedding dress for Masako Owada when she married Prince Naruhito in 1993. But her clothes have been popular not just with Japanese women, but with many rich Europeans and Americans as well, including film stars like Grace Kelly and Sharon Stone and presidents' wives like Nancy Reagan and Hillary Clinton.

Just like Coco Chanel, Hanae also understood that success in fashion could lead to success in other industries. Chanel had shown that when people bought a bottle of perfume, they were buying more than a liquid with a nice smell. The success of Chanel No. 5 showed that people wanted perfume with a stylish image; they wanted perfume with a special name in a special bottle and they were happy to pay a lot of extra money for this.

*Hanae Mori mixes Eastern and Western
ideas in her designs.*

When Hanae Mori produced her own perfume, she knew that customers would connect the stylish image of her clothes with the image of the perfume. She also realized that women, especially women in Japan, would trust her.

'For the first time it's a Japanese woman talking to Japanese women,' she said.

But unlike Coco Chanel, Hanae Mori wanted to do more than just sell designer clothes and perfume. She also saw that she could use her name to sell children's clothes, as well as books and magazines. In fact, Hanae discovered that her famous name and her skill in business could help her in many different areas. When she visited a famous restaurant in Paris, she liked it so much that she decided to start a similar French restaurant in Tokyo. Of course, it was a big success.

Hanae's business now makes over $5 billion a year, and in some ways it seems like a typical international company. Thousands of people work for Hanae, and her head office is in a beautiful, modern glass building in the fashionable area of Omotesando in Tokyo. But her company is still a family business. Her husband, Ken, was involved in the financial side of her business from the early days. He died in 1996, but now her sons and their wives hold important positions in the company. Some of her grandchildren have also started to work in parts of her international operation.

Hanae is now over seventy years old, and she still flies regularly between Tokyo, Paris and New York to check all her different business interests. But when she decides to leave business life, it seems certain that the Hanae Mori tradition will continue. Her ideas will be remembered not just by her family and colleagues, but also by other successful Japanese designers like Issey Miyake, Rei Kawakubo and Yohji Yamamoto. They learned a lot from her because, with her mix of East and West, Hanae was the first Japanese designer to become an international success. She will also be remembered by other Japanese businesswomen. Japan has changed in many ways since Hanae was a bored housewife in the 1940s, but even today there are fewer women in top jobs in Japan than in other big rich countries. Hanae Mori's life shows younger businesswomen that it is always possible to reach the top.

Anita Roddick

Chapter 3   Anita Roddick

'*Business is not about financial language. It is just about buying and
selling and making a magical place where buyer and seller come together.*'
Anita Roddick

Just outside Littlehampton in the south of England, there is a large
modern office building that is built in a Chinese style. It is
specially designed so it does very little damage to the
environment. Its electric power comes from the wind and it
produces very little waste. Inside, some people are discussing the
company's financial performance or its latest sales figures. But
others are discussing campaigns to save the forests of Brazil or
ways of helping political prisoners. Many of them have children
who spend the day playing with teachers in a special area on
another floor while their parents are working. These offices may
be very different from the normal offices of a large international
company, but the people here manage a business with over 1,750
shops in around 50 different countries.

This building is the head office of The Body Shop, a company
which was started by one woman, Anita Roddick, in 1976. In
just a few years, her company has grown from one small shop
into a large international business. During this time, she has
shown people that business is not just about making money; she
believes that business can help to make the world a better place.
And Anita Roddick has also changed the cosmetics industry in a
big way.

Before The Body Shop, cosmetics were sold for high prices in
expensive bottles and packages, but Anita has always tried to sell
cosmetics cheaply and simply. Before The Body Shop, cosmetics
companies rarely used natural ingredients in their products, but

Anita has changed that as well. Before The Body Shop, cosmetics companies always had expensive offices in big, rich cities like Paris or New York, but Anita manages her international business from a small English town.

Littlehampton is beside the sea on the south coast of England and it used to be a popular place for English people to spend their holidays. Anita grew up there in the 1940s and 1950s, and her first experience of business was helping her mother in the busy kitchen of her café. But Anita never thought about a life as a businesswoman. When she left school, she studied to be a teacher and then decided to travel. She visited many countries, including Tahiti, Australia and South Africa.

Soon after she returned to Littlehampton from her travels, she met a man called Gordon Roddick. They fell in love, got married and had two daughters. But life wasn't easy for them. Gordon didn't have a regular job. When he met Anita, he was a writer, but he had never made very much money from his work. Now they had to earn money for their young family. Anita had learnt a lot about the service industry from her experience in her mother's café and, of course, she also knew Littlehampton well, so she and Gordon decided to go into the hotel business. They borrowed some money and bought a small hotel with just eight bedrooms.

The hotel was soon doing well and so next, the Roddicks decided to buy a restaurant. But Anita and Gordon hadn't realized that a restaurant was such hard work. After three years, they decided that they had had enough.

Late one night, Gordon said to Anita, 'I don't want to do this any more. This is killing us.'

He told her that he had an unusual plan. All his life, he had had a dream: he had always wanted to ride a horse from Buenos Aires to New York. Now he wanted to make that dream come true, while he was still young and healthy. But it meant that he would have to leave Anita and the children for two years.

Anita was surprised by the idea, but she was happy to accept the situation. How, though, was she going to earn money for the next two years? She decided to go into business.

While Gordon prepared for his trip, Anita thought about the kind of business she would like to start. She wanted a business that would give her some time to see her children, so she knew that she wanted to work regular hours.

'Why not open a shop?' she thought. That would allow her to work from nine in the morning to five in the afternoon. But what could she sell? She had to find something that people needed but that they couldn't buy from any other shop. She also wanted to do something that she believed in. She didn't want to make money just to get rich; she wanted to be sure that she was selling a good product and offering a good service.

After some time, she started to think about cosmetics. 'Why is there so little choice for women who want to buy cosmetics?' Anita asked herself. 'The cosmetics companies decide what goes into their bottles, they decide how big the bottles should be and, worst of all, they decide to ask a very high price for them.'

And when Anita found out more, she was really shocked by the price of some cosmetics. She realized that some companies were buying their materials for $1 and then selling them for over $100. Customers were often spending a lot of money on a pretty bottle and a famous name.

'These profits are too high,' she thought. 'I know I can sell cosmetics more cheaply.'

While she was travelling around the world, Anita had seen how women in many countries made cosmetics from natural products. Could she do the same thing for women in Britain? She wrote to several big cosmetics companies and asked if they could help her, but they all thought that she was crazy. After several weeks, she found a chemist who could make these things for her. Anita knew she was in business. Next she borrowed

£4,000 from a bank and rented a shop in Brighton, a big town near Littlehampton. The shop was in a good area, but she discovered that its walls were always wet, so she covered them with dark green paint to hide the marks. Her shops are still painted this colour today. As she was painting, she also thought of a name for her business – The Body Shop.

Anita thought it was a great name for her shop, but some of the other businesses in the area weren't so enthusiastic. A week before her new shop's opening day, she received a letter from a lawyer. The letter said that she had to change its name. In the same street as her new shop, there were two companies that organized funerals. Both these companies believed that a shop called 'The Body Shop' so near to them would be bad for their business.

At first Anita was frightened by the lawyer's letter, but then she decided to use it to help her. She called the local newspaper and told them about the two funeral businesses and their attitude towards a poor young woman who was trying to open her first shop. The newspaper printed her story and Anita never heard from the lawyer or from the funeral companies again. She was also pleased because she got a lot of free advertising for her new shop.

Anita was nervous on the morning that the shop opened. She had fifteen products to sell and she had spent several days putting them into bottles. She knew that the shop needed to take £300 a week. It seemed like a lot of money. But Anita didn't need to worry. On the first morning, her shop was full of people. They had never seen anything like Anita's products before; there were soaps that smelled of apples, rose water perfumes, body butter, and skin creams made from natural oil. By the end of the day, Anita had taken £130. She was very happy.

But Anita didn't relax. She tried everything to make customers visit her shop. One day, she even poured perfume along the street that led to her shop door. She hoped that new customers would follow their noses!

The summer of 1976 was hot in the south of England, and lots of people went to Brighton to lie on the beach and swim in the sea. Many of them heard about The Body Shop and went in to buy cream for their burnt skin and tired feet. After just a few months, Anita was doing so well that she wanted to open another shop. She went to the bank and asked if she could borrow another £4,000. But the bank manager thought that Anita was moving too quickly. 'Wait another year,' he told her, 'and we'll discuss it again then.'

But Anita didn't want to wait and so she spoke to a local businessman called Ian McGlinn about her idea. McGlinn agreed to give Anita £4,000, but he wanted to own half of the business. That seemed fair to Anita and so she wrote to Gordon in South America and told him about her plan. Gordon immediately wrote back, and said 'Don't do it!' But his letter arrived too late. Anita had already got the money from Ian McGlinn and he was now the owner of half of The Body Shop. For him, it was one of the best financial decisions of all time: twenty years later, his half of the company had a value of over £100 million!

But while Anita's business was doing well, on the other side of the world Gordon was facing some serious problems. Less than a year after the start of his journey, his horse died in the mountains of Bolivia and he had to return home. Back in Britain, he took over the financial side of The Body Shop's operations. He started to look for ways in which the company could continue to grow.

One of Anita and Gordon's friends admired their business and asked if she could open a Body Shop too. She could get enough money to start a shop; she wanted products to sell and she wanted to use The Body Shop name. It seemed like an excellent idea to Anita and Gordon. It allowed them to increase the size of their business, but it meant that they didn't have to borrow any more money. When this new Body Shop became successful, they looked for other people who also wanted to open Body Shops. They found plenty of people who thought that this was a great opportunity, and soon Body Shops were opening in towns and cities across the UK. In

*Soon Body Shops were opening in towns
and cities across the UK.*

1978 the first Body Shop opened outside the UK, in Brussels, and the next year the business spread to Sweden and Greece. By 1981, a new Body Shop was opening somewhere in the world every two weeks.

As the business grew, The Body Shop started making more and more different products. People often came to Anita with strange ideas for natural cosmetics that she could use in her business.

One day, an old lady from Vienna arrived at The Body Shop's offices with a bag of white powder. She explained that it was a special skin treatment which her grandfather had prepared for Archduke Ferdinand of Austria many years ago. Anita liked the story and agreed to test the lady's white powder. To her surprise, it really worked, and it later became one of the Body Shop's most successful products. The little old lady returned to Austria to lead a comfortable life, because Anita had promised to give her 10% of all the money that her product made.

In 1984, Anita and Gordon decided that The Body Shop needed even more money so it could continue to grow. They decided to sell shares in the company at the London Stock Exchange. Half of these shares were already owned by Ian McGlinn because he owned half the company as a result of his arrangement with Anita in 1976. Anita and Gordon kept some shares in The Body Shop for themselves and they sold the rest to the public. When the Body Shop shares first went on sale, Anita and Gordon were at the London Stock Exchange to watch. At the start of the day, the share price was £0.95. But as the hours passed, the price went higher as more and more people tried to buy a piece of The Body Shop. When the Stock Exchange finished business that afternoon, the price had risen to £1.65. Anita took out a piece of paper and added some figures together. The value of her own Body Shop shares was £1.5 million. After just eight years in business, at the age of forty-two, Anita Roddick was a millionaire!

◆

The early 1980s was a good time to sell natural products. Several international news stories at that time made people think about the harmful effects of modern industry. Scientists found that the world was getting hotter because of the smoke and gas from factories and cars. They also discovered that in the forests of countries like Brazil, rare plants and animals were quickly disappearing. Then, in December 1984, poisonous gas escaped from a factory in Bhopal, India, and killed 2,000 people. Sixteen months later, there was an explosion at a power station at Chernobyl, Ukraine. A cloud of poison killed many people and caused damage to plants and animals right across Europe. These problems made many people wonder if we should all change our lifestyles. They thought that we should stop using so many dangerous products and start to live in a more natural way.

Anita Roddick understood these ideas. She had always tried to make The Body Shop a clean business that didn't damage the environment. Her cosmetics were made from natural products and she had never allowed people to test her products on animals; instead, they had always been tested on people. She also always asked her customers to use their bottles again, to reduce waste. She believed that business was not just about making a profit, and that companies should act in a responsible way towards society and towards the earth. Because of this, people were happy to shop at The Body Shop if they were worried about the environment.

But Anita wanted to do more than just run a responsible business. She thought that business could give her the opportunity to make the world a better place. So in 1985, she started working with a group called Greenpeace to stop companies putting waste and poisons into the sea. As part of the campaign to keep the seas clean, The Body Shop paid for advertising and gave its customers information about the problem. Over the next few years, The Body Shop worked with other groups on campaigns to save rare animals and to help people who had been wrongly put in prison. In 1989, Anita ran a campaign to stop the burning of trees in the forests of Brazil. The campaigns were a chance for The Body Shop's employees to learn about these problems, and they were all expected to help Anita to make them successful.

Other businesspeople were surprised by Anita's campaigns. The 1980s was a time when many businesspeople were only interested in profit.

'Why does she spend so much time trying to save the world?' they asked. 'She should be in her office, running her business like a normal businesswoman.'

They were even more surprised when she began to fly to some of the poorer places in the world, helping people to start businesses. To some companies, poor countries are just places to buy cheap materials and hire cheap workers. This can often have damaging results for the local society. But Anita believed that her business could help. So she went to the forests of Brazil and worked with the Kayapo people. The Kayapo had lived according to their old traditions for thousands of years. But now, changes in the modern world meant that it was difficult for their way of life to continue. Anita helped them to start a business that produced oil for cosmetics. They could make this from plants that they found in the forest and then sell it to The Body Shop for a good price. The Kayapo were happy because they now had money to pay for better health and education; it was also good for The Body Shop, because Anita had another natural product to sell. After her success with the Kayapo, Anita used the same kind of idea to help poor people in many other parts of the world.

Although Anita spent a lot of time and energy on her campaigns and her work for the poor, her business certainly didn't suffer. Every year, more Body Shops opened, more customers bought her products and the company's profits grew bigger.

But some people said that Anita's campaigns weren't really about saving the world. They were just a way to get cheap advertising and to make the company look good in the eyes of its customers. In 1994, some newspapers and television programmes went further. They criticized The Body Shop and said that it hadn't done enough to protect the environment. Customers were worried and the company's share price suddenly fell. Anita and Gordon were very angry. They felt that they had always been honest and that the criticism was not fair. Gordon had a meeting with journalists and told them, 'The company doesn't pretend to be perfect or to have all the answers, but it can still help in the fight to protect the environment.' The Body Shop's customers were happy to believe him. Soon they were back in the shops, and the company's share price was going up again.

In recent years, Anita has become less involved in the business side of The Body Shop's activities. In 1998, she decided that she wanted someone else to take control of the day-to-day management of the company and a man called Patrick Gournay was brought from France to become The Body Shop's boss. Anita stayed with the company, but recently she has told the world that she is thinking of leaving business life. She said that she didn't want to spend her whole life talking about skin creams and soaps, because she had more important things to do: she wanted to get involved in more political campaigns.

Anita once said that there were no heroes in the modern business world, but she has certainly become a hero for many people. She has shown that it is possible for a woman to build a large international company in just a few years. She has proved that it is possible to manage a business and care for the environment at the same time. And she has brought new ideas, new products and new life to the world's shopping centres.

Chapter 4   Oprah Winfrey

'*I will never, never, as long as I'm black, I will never give up my power to another person.*'

Oprah Winfrey

One morning in 1990, seventeen million Americans were, as usual, watching *The Oprah Winfrey Show* on TV. Oprah was talking to four ordinary people who had all had problems at work. They each told a story of greedy companies, selfish bosses and lazy colleagues, while Oprah asked them questions, smiled and listened carefully. Many of the stories were familiar to the people across the US who were watching Oprah's show. Oprah's viewers were mostly ordinary Americans, and many of them had experienced similar problems in their offices, shops and factories. To these people, Oprah was one of them. She had come from a poor family and she had had a tough childhood. She had had to fight for everything in her life. Oprah seemed to be someone who had suffered the same problems as they had and who saw things in the same way.

So everyone was looking forward to some fun when Oprah introduced her next guest. He was a writer on business called Harvey McKay. You could see immediately that McKay would be on the side of the bosses. He would try to explain why they often behaved badly towards ordinary workers. He would try to explain why the bosses earned such a lot of money, while ordinary people earned so little. And then Oprah would have her chance to ask him a few difficult questions. She would tell him how ordinary people felt about big business.

But Harvey McKay surprised everyone. He didn't just talk and give answers; he started asking Oprah questions about her life.

Oprah Winfrey

'It seems to me,' he said to her after a few minutes, 'that you're a tough but fair boss.'

Oprah looked pleased and called to the people who helped her at the back of the stage, 'I'm very fair, aren't I, girls?'

For many of Oprah's viewers, this was an interesting moment. They had watched her shows every day for many years and they thought they knew most things about her. They had heard about her problems as a child whose parents had separated. They had listened to her tell them about her relationships. They even knew what she ate and that she had often tried to lose weight. But Oprah was also a boss, and that idea was new and interesting to many of them. When they thought about it, it was clear that Oprah was much more than just a friendly woman on a popular talk show.

Oprah didn't just appear on *The Oprah Winfrey Show* – she owned *The Oprah Winfrey Show*. That meant that she earned a lot of money from the advertisements in the breaks in the programme. She also owned the studios where they made her show. It was one of the best TV production centres in the US, and it had cost around $20 million. In fact, her company, Harpo Productions, gave Oprah control over her life and over the lives of many other people. In the entertainment business, Oprah's love of control was famous; although she was very busy, she signed every cheque for her company, so she always knew exactly how every cent was spent.

◆

It was perhaps strange that Oprah had become so interested in controlling her life; she had started in talk shows because she was so out of control. Her first jobs were as a newsreader for small radio and TV stations in the south of the US in the early 1970s. In those days, it was quite unusual for Americans to see a black woman reading the TV news, and in 1976 she was offered a job with a much bigger TV station in the city of Baltimore. Everyone thought she looked great on TV, but she didn't have the right character to be a good journalist. She always became too involved in the stories. When stories were sad, she sometimes started to cry. When the stories were happy, she was clearly happy too.

'This is crazy,' her bosses said. 'We have to find this woman another job.'

At the time, the TV station wanted to introduce a morning talk show; this would give the people of Baltimore a chance to appear on TV and discuss their opinions. The show was called *People Are Talking*. As Oprah clearly understood people so well, perhaps she would be the right person to present this programme. It could be a much better use of her skills than reading the news.

Many TV interviewers prepare questions before an interview and then don't really listen to the answers of their guests during the show. But Oprah was very different. She was always interested in what people said. She had real conversations with the people that she interviewed. Soon, her bosses in Baltimore realized that Oprah was a star.

Oprah's show was so successful that, after a few years, TV bosses in other parts of the country started to notice her. In 1983, a big TV station in Chicago asked her to present their morning talk show, *A.M. Chicago*. They offered her a four-year contract and said that they would pay her $200,000 a year. It was a lot of money, but Oprah was worried about moving to Chicago. She didn't need to be, because when she arrived there she immediately felt at home.

'Just walking down the street, I knew I belonged there,' she said.

And the people of Chicago also felt that she belonged to them. Her talk show started in January 1984, and it was an immediate hit. People loved her direct, personal style of interviewing and, within a few months, her programme was the most popular morning show in the city. Her boss at the TV station was very happy. 'Oprah hit Chicago like a bucket of cold water,' he said. 'She just took over the town.'

Oprah was a star in one of the biggest cities in the US, but she now wanted to become a national star. Her opportunity came when she got a call from Steven Spielberg. Spielberg was one of the most important people in the Hollywood film industry; he had made several successful films, including *E.T.* He now wanted to make a film of a book by the black American writer, Alice Walker, called *The Color Purple*.

'Would you like to play a part in the film?' he asked her.

Oprah couldn't refuse. *The Color Purple* was one of her favourite books, and she also knew that a part in a Hollywood film would make her famous around the world. But she was so busy with *A.M. Chicago* that she had no time to do any other work. Oprah wanted to be in the film so much that she was ready to leave her job with the TV station. But her business manager, Jeffrey Jacobs, had other ideas.

'We can work this out,' he told her. 'The TV station will have to give you a break from the show.'

Oprah's bosses weren't very happy about the situation, but they didn't want to lose her and they could also see that the film could bring a lot of public attention to her show. They agreed to give her a break of several weeks so she could work on *The Color Purple*.

Oprah was very grateful to the TV station, but the experience also helped her to see that there were a few problems with her present contract. If she really wanted to become a star, she needed more control over her life. But how could she get this?

Jeffrey Jacobs realized that if Oprah wanted to control her life, she first needed to get control of her programme. At that time it was only broadcast in the Chicago area, but he thought that it should be possible to broadcast it right across the country. He knew that when *The Color Purple* arrived in the cinemas, Oprah was going to become an international star. Lots of people outside Chicago would want to see her show.

Oprah decided to negotiate with the TV station. First, she made them change the name of the programme to *The Oprah Winfrey Show*. Then she asked for a share of the money from sales of her show to other TV stations. It was a great business decision. When *The Color Purple* came out, the film was a big success and everybody admired Oprah's performance. As a result, they all wanted to watch her TV show too. One hundred and thirty eight TV stations across the US bought *The Oprah Winfrey Show*, and suddenly her earnings jumped from \$200,000 a year to \$30 million a year!

Oprah's decision had made her rich, and it had also taught her an important lesson: control was the key to success. So in 1986 she started her own company, called Harpo Productions. ('Harpo' is 'Oprah' spelled backwards.) At first, it was just to create publicity for her show and to answer letters from viewers, but Oprah had big plans for her new company. In 1988, she started to negotiate with the bosses of the Chicago TV station again. This time she wanted Harpo Productions to buy *The Oprah Winfrey Show* from them. The TV station bosses weren't happy. They knew that Harpo would still allow them to broadcast the show, but the deal meant that they were losing control of their most important programme. As negotiations continued it became clear that, if necessary, Oprah was prepared to walk away from her show and go to work in Hollywood. The TV station bosses realized they had no choice; they had to give Oprah what she wanted.

As she now owned her own show, Oprah needed a place where she could record it. So she bought an old TV and film production centre in west Chicago for \$10 million. She then spent another \$10 million on new equipment to make sure that

Oprah in The Color Purple

Harpo Studios was the best production centre in the city. Oprah could now make her shows at times which suited her and she could also make more money from them. But her studio allowed her to do much more than that. In 1988, Harpo Productions started making other programmes for TV, like *The Women Of Brewster Place,* and soon other companies were using Harpo Studios to make advertisements, films and TV shows.

In the 1990s, Oprah's business continued to expand in many different areas of the entertainment industry. Ordinary people, especially American women, trust her and understand her ideas and beliefs. They see her as an honest person from a tough background who has fought for her success. This means that many people are happy to buy products that carry Oprah's name. This has given Oprah many great business opportunities. In 1998 she created a company called Oxygen Media, which produces TV programmes for women and children and makes similar material for the Internet. Recently, she also started work on a new women's magazine, and she even has her own film company which has signed a contract with Disney.

When Oprah had her fortieth birthday in January 1994, she was already the most powerful woman in the world's entertainment industry and also the most highly paid. Over the past few years, business magazines have regularly put her in their lists of top American businesswomen. At the same time, *The Oprah Winfrey Show* has continued to be as successful as ever – not just in the US, but also in many other countries around the world. Because Oprah is now in control of her life, she has also found time to act in several more Hollywood films. And as her business has grown, Oprah has become richer and richer. It now seems likely that she will become America's first black billionaire.

Chapter 5   Madonna

'*Life is short. My idea is that if I want to do something, I do it.*'
Madonna

Most pop stars know that they don't have a job for life. One or two successful records may give them enough money to have a good time for a few months. But the days of fast cars and long hot days by the swimming pool don't last long. Most have returned to ordinary life by the time they are thirty.

But Madonna isn't like that. She has been the world's top female pop star since the middle of the 1980s. During that time she has had many hit records, she has acted in several films, and she has made millions and millions of dollars. She has won prizes for her work, but she has also been strongly criticized by politicians and religious leaders. She has married, separated and married again. She has had two children and she has also shocked a lot of people with her wild behaviour.

Some people say that she has been successful for such a long time just because she is a wonderful singer and songwriter, but most agree that it isn't as simple as that. Madonna has always made sure that she is in control of her life. She has made careful plans and has cleverly used the publicity that surrounds her. She has also used her success to build a large international company that makes big profits.

◆

But Madonna started right at the bottom. When nineteen-year-old Madonna Ciccone arrived in New York City in 1978, she knew that she wanted to be rich and she knew that she wanted to be a star. But she came from an ordinary family in a town called

Madonna

Pontiac in Michigan, and she had just $35 in her purse. New York is no place for someone with no money, so her first years in the city were very tough. She lived in rooms in some of the worst areas, and she did all kinds of jobs to make money. Sometimes she worked as an artist's model or a dancer. Sometimes she worked in restaurants and bars. But there were also days when she was so poor that she had to get her food from rubbish bags in the street.

During this difficult time, Madonna never forgot her dream of becoming a star. When she wasn't earning money, she learnt to sing and play musical instruments. She also taught herself to write music. Soon she was writing and recording her own songs. In 1982, someone at a record company listened to her song 'Everybody' and decided to offer her a recording contract. It seemed that her dream had come true.

But Madonna quickly realized that she still had a long way to go. 'Everybody' was a dance song and it was popular in the nightclubs of New York, but most people in the US and the rest of the world didn't notice it. This wasn't good enough for Madonna. She wanted to find a way of getting everybody to buy 'Everybody'!

◆

In the days of Elvis Presley, The Beatles and The Rolling Stones, the music industry had been mainly about making music and selling records. Pop stars were rarely seen on TV, so most people listened to the radio to hear the latest songs from the pop world. But in the early 1980s, that started to change. In 1981, an American TV company called MTV (Music Television) started to broadcast pop videos to teenagers and young people across the US. Their first song was 'Video Killed The Radio Star' by the British group, The Buggles. It was a perfect way to start, because the song's words told the story of the future of the industry. Over the next few months, across the US, more and more teenagers switched off their radios and turned on MTV. Soon MTV had spread to a hundred countries around the world. The pop music industry became more international than ever before. Record companies realized that a good song needed a good video to become a hit. Because of this, they started to look for singers with their own style who could perform well on video.

Madonna knew that she could be this kind of star. She didn't just have great songs and a great voice. She also had her own way of dancing and her own way of dressing. She had had some success in New York, but how could she now become a star on the world stage?

She decided that she needed a manager to help her. Because she was Madonna, an ordinary manager wasn't good enough; she needed the best manager in the business. At that time, many people thought that the best manager in the pop music industry was Freddy Demann. He had worked with Michael Jackson for several years and had helped him to produce some of the most successful records of all time. Demann understood how to make videos, and he knew how to work with MTV. So Madonna just had to persuade him to work with her. But how?

In Madonna's position, most young singers sent a manager a letter and a recording of their songs. But Madonna wanted to be different. She found out Freddy Demann's address, walked straight into his office and performed her songs in front of him. Freddy was rather surprised, but he also liked what he heard and what he saw.

'She had that special magic that very few stars have,' he said.

Freddy Demann was the right man for her. Her next song, 'Holiday', was also a dance song, but it wasn't just a hit in New York. It was a hit on MTV; it was a hit across America; it was a hit right around the world. Freddy also found an opportunity for her to act in a Hollywood film. By the end of 1984, she wasn't just a radio star; she wasn't just a video star; she was a film star as well!

♦

In the middle years of the 1980s, money and success seemed to be the most important things in the world. The American economy was doing very well and President Ronald Reagan had reduced taxes, so people in business had a lot of money to spend. In New York, young businesswomen wore big diamonds and beautiful dresses from the world's top designers, and they loved to drive to parties in expensive foreign cars. Intelligent people from outside the business world were often asked, 'If you're so clever, why aren't you rich?' There was no answer to that.

During those years, Madonna's face was always in the newspapers, her videos were always on MTV and her songs were everywhere. She had one hit record after another. One of her songs from 1985 seemed to explain the feeling of the time. 'We are living in a material world,' she sang. 'And I am a material girl.'

Madonna had always wanted to be a public figure, but her boyfriend in the middle years of the 1980s had very different ideas. Sean Penn was a film star who had grown up in a famous family and, perhaps because of that, he hated newspaper photographers. This was a problem, because photographers followed Madonna everywhere. At first, Sean tried to push them away. But when they didn't stay away, he hit them. And when they still didn't stay away, he tried to frighten them with his guns. When Sean and Madonna got married in 1985, the newspapers sent helicopters so they could photograph the wedding. This was too much for Sean; he left the party and shot at them with his gun from the ground. In the end, Sean's problems with the newspapers caused too many problems and he was sent to prison. Madonna separated from him after just a few years of marriage.

It was a hard lesson in the problems that come from too much public attention. But Madonna was one of the most famous women in the world and she loved the publicity. So when the drinks company Pepsi-Cola asked her to do an advertising campaign for them, she was happy to help. She negotiated with them for eight months and she was even happier when they agreed to pay her $5 million for a year's contract.

On 2 March, 1989, Madonna's Pepsi advertisement was broadcast to around 250 million people in forty countries, and it included part of her new song 'Like a Prayer'. The advertisement was great, but it was never seen again. That was because on 3 March, MTV showed Madonna's own 'Like a Prayer' video. This showed Madonna in all sorts of strange situations inside a church. Religious people around the world were very angry with Madonna.

'How dare she use our religion like this?' they asked.

After some time, things got so bad that the Pope said that Madonna would not be welcome to perform in Italy. The people at Pepsi-Cola were very worried about the situation. Would this damage their sales? They didn't want to wait to find out. They decided not to use Madonna's advertisement again, although they let her keep their $5 million. But Madonna was the winner in another way as well. After all the talk about 'Like a Prayer' in the newspapers and on TV, everybody wanted to buy the record. It soon became a best-seller in thirty countries around the world.

After 'Like a Prayer', some people began to see Madonna in a new way. They realized that she wasn't just an ordinary pop star. She had been at the top of her business for a long time; she was clearly a very tough person. In October 1990, the American business magazine *Forbes* put Madonna's picture on its front cover and asked if she was the cleverest businesswoman in the US. It said that she had earned $39 million over the past year. It also said that she was very unusual because she was a star who ran her own business. The next month, *Us* magazine produced a list of the most powerful people in the entertainment industry.

Madonna was at number one, above stars like Michael Jackson, Bruce Springsteen and Prince.

In 1992, she proved her skills as a businesswoman when she signed a deal with a value of $60 million with the big entertainment company Time Warner. The deal meant that she was now the boss of her own company, called Maverick. Maverick could produce records, videos, TV programmes and books, and it gave Madonna complete control over her own products.

She used this control to surprise everybody again. Maverick's first product was not a record or even a video; it was a book of photographs called *Sex*. The book was unusual in many ways. Its cover was made of metal and it contained a CD of a new Madonna song. It also contained photographs that showed Madonna without her clothes on. In the weeks before *Sex* arrived in bookshops, journalists around the world wrote about the book. Many people thought she was making a big mistake. But Madonna was completely confident. She decided to print a million copies of the book and to sell it for a very high price – nearly $50.

When the book finally went on sale in October 1992, the big question at every fashionable party was, 'Have you seen the Madonna *Sex* book?' Some people were shocked by Madonna's photographs, others were angry, but many just went out and bought it. It sold 500,000 copies in its first week!

But Maverick was not just an opportunity for Madonna to produce and sell her own books, records and videos; it also meant that she could work with other young musicians.

'I want a real record label with real artists,' she said. 'I want artists who have a life of their own and who have a point of view.'

Since 1992, Madonna and her team of managers have listened to hundreds of recordings from young singers as they have tried

Canadian singer and songwriter,
Alanis Morisette.

to find the stars of the future. Everyone in the music industry agrees that this is very hard to do. Sadly, most young musicians fail. But Madonna quickly showed that she could find the right people and, in 1995, Maverick produced a record by the Canadian singer and songwriter, Alanis Morisette. She was a good choice; her record sold over 27 million copies around the world! Maverick has also made records for hit films like *Austin Powers* and *The Next Best Thing*. In 1999, the company had sales of around $750 million.

Madonna's busy life means that she can't spend a lot of time in her company's offices like a normal boss. But wherever she goes, she uses the Internet to communicate with her company's managers who look after the business from day to day.

Madonna is certainly not everyone's idea of a typical businessperson; she will always be best known for her songs, her films and her shocking way of life. But as computers, better communications and the internet change business, ideas and style are becoming much more important than machines and materials. If you want to succeed in the twenty-first century, you need to be able to think of new products and new fashions, and you must also know how to use publicity and how to create the right image. In the factories and offices of the old business world, the bosses were nearly always serious men in dark suits and ties. But in today's business world, women are proving that they are better managers and that they know more about the lives of ordinary people. In the expensive designer shops of Chanel and Hanae Mori, in the hundreds of Body Shops, and in the studios of Harpo and Maverick, the message is clear: modern women mean business!

Business Wordlist

accountant	a person who reports the financial health of an organization
branch	a part of a large organization, often a store or an office
capital	money that helps to build a new business
compete	to try to win
consultant	a person who gives business advice
contract	a formal legal agreement
corporation	a big company
deal	to buy and sell
expand	to increase or grow
finances	the amount of money that a business or person has
industry	a type of business
loss	the amount of money that a business loses
negotiate	to try to come to an agreement with another person
objective	a business aim
partnership	a business that is owned by two or more people
profit	money that is made in business
risk	the danger of losing money
sack	to tell someone to leave their job
share	a piece of paper that says that you own part of a company
stock exchange	a place where people buy and sell shares

ACTIVITIES

Chapter 1

Before you read

1   Why is Coco Chanel famous? What products did she make?
2   Find the words in *italics* in your dictionary. They are used in this book. Which are words for
    a   people?
    b   beauty products?
    archduke   cosmetics   lawyer   perfume
3   Discuss these questions. Check the meanings of the words in *italics*.
    a   Do you look for beautiful *designs* when you buy clothes? Why (not)?
    b   Do advertisements *persuade* you to buy things? Why (not)?
    c   When do you wear *smart* clothes? Why?
    d   How important is it to be *tough* in business?

After you read

4   Answer these questions about Coco Chanel.
    a   How did she get the money for her first shop?
    b   Why was the First World War good for her business?
    c   How did her business change in the 1920s?
    d   How successful was she in Hollywood? What was the reason for this?
    e   How did she spend her time during the Second World War?
    f   Why did she live in Switzerland for many years? How did she make money during this time?
    g   Why did she return to the fashion business at the age of seventy?

Chapter 2

Before you read

5   What do you know about the situation for working women in Japan? Is it easy for women to become successful there?

6 Answer these questions. Find the words in *italics* in your dictionary.

   a When you are *involved*, are you busy or not?

   b If someone has a tough *image*, are they tough or do they look tough?

   c If something is *obvious*, is it easy or difficult to understand?

   d Do you *trust* your friends or your enemies?

After you read

  7 Answer these questions about Hanae Mori.

   a Who did she meet in 1961, and why was this meeting important in her life?

   b Who were her most important customers in the 1950s?

   c How did the designer fashion industry change in the 1960s and 1970s?

   d What is special about Hanae's style?

   e What business interests does she have outside the fashion industry?

Chapter 3

Before you read

  8 Have you ever been to The Body Shop? What kinds of products did you see there?

  9 Find these words in your dictionary.

   campaign   environment   funeral   ingredients   millionaire
   powder   rise   take over

   Which word means

   a a very rich person?

   b the world around us?

   c to take control?

   d a number of events which have the same objective?

   e an event to remember a dead person?

   f dust?

   g things which you put together to make other things?

   h to go up?

After you read

10 Answer these questions about Anita Roddick.

   a Why did she decide to go into business?

   b What was different about The Body Shop's cosmetics?

   c What did Ian McGlinn do for The Body Shop?

   d What part of the business did Gordon Roddick control?

   e How did Anita become a millionaire in 1984?

   e Why were the 1980s good years to sell natural cosmetics?

   f How did The Body Shop help the Kayapo people?

   g Why did journalists criticize The Body Shop in the early 1990s?

Chapter 4

Before you read

11 Have you ever seen *The Oprah Winfrey Show*? What kind of image does Oprah Winfrey have? Does she act like a top businesswoman?

12 Make sentences with the words below. Find these words in your dictionary.

   a *billionaire*   a *hit*   *studio*

   b *create*   *direct* (adj)   *publicity*

After you read

13 Answer these questions about Oprah Winfrey.

   a Why wasn't Oprah a success as a newsreader?

   b Why was it difficult for Oprah to appear in *The Color Purple*?

   c Why did Oprah's earnings suddenly increase to $30 million a year?

   d How did Harpo persuade the TV company to sell *The Oprah Winfrey Show*?

   e How has Oprah's business expanded over recent years?

Chapter 5

Before you read

14 What do you already know about Madonna? What kind of person is she?

15 Answer these questions. Find the words in *italics* in your dictionary.

    a What kind of places do you go to in a *helicopter*?

    b What kind of things does a *material* girl like?

    c People say that you can be too rich. What is your *point of view*?

    d Which *record label* produces your favourite pop group?

After you read

16 Make notes in two lists.

    a What did you know about Madonna before you read this chapter?

    b What have you learnt about her from this book?

17 Which other famous women in business do you know? What companies or products are they famous for?

Writing

18 Write a one- or two-line description of the power of each businesswoman in this book.

19 Write a short newspaper report. Compare Coco Chanel and Hanae Mori. Write about how they are different and how they are similar.

20 Write a letter to Anita Roddick. Ask her for a job at The Body Shop and explain why you would like to work for the company.

21 You are going to interview Oprah Winfrey about her life as a businesswoman. Write a list of ten questions that you would like to ask her.

22 Write a letter to Madonna. Describe one of your favourite groups or singers and persuade her to offer them a recording contract with Maverick.

23 Write a short report explaining how a person with a famous name can use this to sell products. Use at least two examples from this book.